D0679463

International Cooking Collection

Microwave Cooking

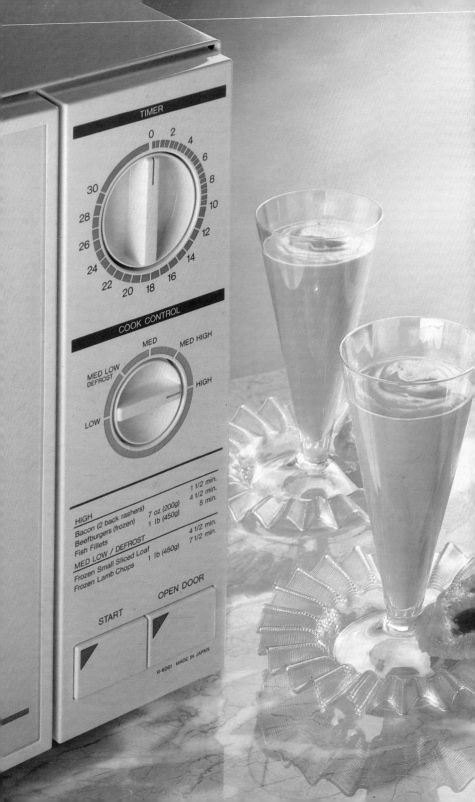

International
Cooking Collection

Microwave
Cooking

Lorna Rhodes

CONTENTS

Published exclusively for Cupress (Canada) Ltd
20 Torbay Road, Markham, Ontario L3R 1G6 Canada
by Woodhead-Faulkner (Publishers) Ltd, Simon & Schuster International Group

This edition first published 1988
© Woodhead-Faulkner (Publishers) Ltd 1988
ISBN 0–920691–56–0
Printed and bound in Italy

INTRODUCTION

If you already own a microwave oven and have followed the basic cooking methods given in the manufacturer's handbook, you will have discovered all the advantages of microwave cooking. It defrosts and cooks quickly, reheats, without drying the food, and creates less washing-up. It is clean to use, convenient to place in the kitchen, but most of all it cooks many foods perfectly, retaining the flavors and textures of foods such as fish and vegetables and minimizing the loss of nutrients which often occurs in other cooking methods.

More and more people are being attracted to microwave cooking, particularly those who do not like spending time in the kitchen, and those who enjoy cooking but have not got the time. Microwave ovens are so easy to use and so much safer than a conventional oven that they are ideal for older people who may cook only small amounts of food and for the disabled who can place it at a comfortable level. There are also considerable savings in fuel consumption because meals can be produced in only a quarter or fifth of the normal cooking time and the microwave oven uses less power than a conventional oven. The kitchen stays cooler and windows do not get steamed up.

RECIPE GUIDELINES

The recipes in this book will show you just how versatile microwave cooking can be. Tables giving defrosting and cooking times for individual food items are not given as these will be found in your handbooks. Most of the cooking methods suitable for a microwave are used in the recipes, and the variety of dishes will be sure to please both family and friends.

The wattage of your microwave oven will determine how long food takes to cook. All these recipes have been tested on a 650 watt microwave oven with a turntable. For a 500 watt microwave oven increase the cooking time by about 40 seconds for every minute given and for a 600 watt oven increase the cooking time by 20 seconds per minute. For a 700 watt oven decrease the time by 20 seconds per minute.

Most microwave ovens now have a variable power control which may be described as HIGH, MEDIUM and LOW; or may be referred to as FULL POWER, ROAST, SIMMER, DEFROST and WARM; or it could be described as % of full power. Whichever control your oven has, the highest setting will be equivalent to FULL POWER or 100 per cent energy output.

FULL POWER is used for most general high-speed cooking methods, for instance when cooking fish, vegetables, fruits, hot drinks, bacon, preheating the browning dish and melting butter. It is the *only* setting available on basic on/off microwave models.

MEDIUM POWER is used primarily for baking, roasting, cooking casseroles and for reheating previously cooked foods. Foods retain more moisture on MEDIUM, and reducing the power means less stirring and watching.

LOW POWER is used for defrosting and simmering, softening butter and it is the setting used for very gentle cooking.

A GUIDE TO COMPARATIVE CONTROL SETTINGS

Descriptions used in this book	HIGH	MEDIUM	LOW	DEFROST
Other comparable descriptions used	FULL	ROAST BAKE	SIMMER STEW	DEFROST
	7	6–5	4–3	2
APPROXIMATE POWER OUTPUT	100%	50%–60%	30%	20%

TIMING

Timing is very important in microwave cooking—overcooking will dry out the food and make it tough. It is always better to undercook the food, as it can be returned to the oven for a while longer if necessary. Microwave models vary greatly, so to ensure you do not overcook food, check it well before due time.

As the food is cooked so quickly, it will retain a great deal of heat after it has been taken out of the oven and will continue to cook. This has been taken into account in the recipes and it is another reason why it is most important to observe the times.

If a standing time is given in a recipe, cover the food with foil when it is removed from the oven and leave to stand for the time indicated. If for any reason after this period the food requires additional microwave time, it can be cooked a little longer, but the standing time does not need to be repeated.

The times given in these recipes are specific to the quantity of food being cooked. If you alter the amounts given in the recipe, the cooking time will need to be adapted. In general, when doubling the amount of food, increase the cooking time by one third to one half.

When planning to cook a whole meal in your microwave oven, remember that most meat, fish and poultry dishes improve upon standing and can be reheated quickly. Those foods which require standing time should therefore be cooked first, and quick-cooking dishes cooked during that standing time.

COOKING EQUIPMENT

For general all-round use, glass, pottery and china can be used in the microwave; check that the dishes do not have a metallic rim.

For shorter cooking periods, paper cookware, waxed paper, paper towels and cardboard can be used. Plastic is ideal for short cooking times, as are cooking and roasting bags. However plastic should never be used for mixtures which become extremely hot during cooking. So avoid plastic containers for heating combinations of sugar and fat, or sugar and water, otherwise the container may be damaged.

Special microwave equipment is available, such as defrost boxes, microwave thermometers (specially made without mercury), and various shaped cookware made in durable plastic. Browning skillets have a special non-stick coating which absorbs microwave energy. When preheated, the skillets become hot and can then be used to brown and seal chops, chicken portions and joints of meat prior to roasting.

COVERING FOOD

Whenever a recipe states 'cover', use either the lids provided with the microwave containers or microwave-safe plastic wrap placed over the dish. If using plastic wrap, make sure that it does not come into direct contact with the food and pierce it in two places with a small sharp knife to allow steam to escape and so prevent ballooning.

HELPFUL HINTS

- Always use ovengloves to remove dishes from the microwave oven as they can be quite hot.
- Do not overload the oven, or its speed and efficiency will be impaired.
- For foods that should contain moisture, always cover the container when cooking on HIGH. The cover should not be completely airtight for long cooking times: if using plastic wrap, stretch it over the dish and then fold back one corner.
- After cooking, peel back the plastic wrap from the far side of the dish to avoid steam burns.
- Use the oven to freshen up stale coffee beans.
- Soak 1 envelope gelatin in water until spongy, then microwave on HIGH for 1 minute or until clear.
- Place herbs and citrus rinds on a plate and microwave on HIGH until dry. Cool and store in containers.
- Microwave butter on LOW for 1 minute to soften.
- Prick the skins of citrus fruits and microwave on HIGH for 10 seconds to gain maximum juice when squeezed.
- Break chocolate into a bowl and microwave on MEDIUM for 1 minute per oz to melt.
- Microwave nuts on HIGH for 4–5 minutes, until lightly brown, stirring twice.

NOTES

All spoon measurements are level.

All recipes have been tested on 650 watt microwave ovens. Models with different power levels can be used by making adjustments to cooking times (see page 5).

Freshly ground black pepper is intended where pepper is listed.

Fresh herbs are used unless otherwise stated. If unobtainable dried herbs can be substituted in cooked dishes but halve the quantities.

Use U.S. grade large eggs unless otherwise stated.

Always follow your microwave oven manufacturer's operating instructions and recommendations.

CURRIED PARSNIP SOUP

2 tablespoons butter or margarine
1 small onion, chopped
3¼ cups thinly sliced parsnips

2 teaspoons mild curry powder
4½ cups hot chicken stock
salt and pepper to taste
snipped chives to garnish

Serves 4
Preparation time:
10 minutes
Power setting:
HIGH
Cooking time:
21 minutes

1. Place the butter or margarine in a large bowl and microwave on HIGH for 1 minute. Add the onion and parsnips, then cover and cook on HIGH for 3 minutes.
2. Stir in the curry powder and cook on HIGH for 2 minutes.
3. Pour in the stock, season with salt and pepper, then cover and cook on HIGH for 15 minutes or until the parsnips are tender.
4. Put the soup into a blender or food processor and work until smooth. Garnish with snipped chives and serve immediately, with crusty bread.

TOMATO AND CARROT SOUP

√

2 tablespoons butter
1 onion, chopped
1¼ cups thinly sliced carrots
4 medium-size ripe tomatoes, skinned and chopped

1 teaspoon sugar
2½ cups hot vegetable stock
rosemary sprig
salt and pepper to taste
flat-leaved parsley to garnish

Serves 4
Preparation time:
15 minutes
Power setting:
HIGH
Cooking time:
26 minutes

1. Place the butter in a large bowl and microwave on HIGH for 1 minute. Add the onion and carrot and cooks for 5 minutes.
2. Add the tomatoes, sugar, stock and rosemary to the bowl, cover and cook on HIGH for 18 minutes.
3. Remove the rosemary, then pour the soup into a blender or food processor and work until smooth. Season with salt and pepper, then return to the bowl and cook on HIGH for 2 minutes.
4. Garnish with parsley to serve.

CREAMY WATERCRESS SOUP

This fresh-tasting soup can be served chilled for a summer meal or hot with croutons.

¹/₄ cup butter
2 large bunches watercress, chopped
1 onion, chopped
2¹/₂ cups hot vegetable stock

1 teaspoon lemon juice
2 tablespoons cornstarch
1¹/₄ cups milk
pinch of grated nutmeg
salt and pepper to taste
¹/₄ cup whipping cream

Serves 4
Preparation time:
10 minutes
Power setting:
HIGH
Cooking time:
16 minutes

1. Place the butter in a large bowl and microwave on HIGH for 1 minute. Add the watercress and onion, cover the bowl and cook for 5 minutes.
2. Add the stock, lemon juice, and salt and pepper, cover the bowl and cook on HIGH for 5 minutes.
3. Cool a little, then pour into a blender or food processor and work until smooth.
4. Blend the cornstarch with a little of the milk to a smooth paste, then stir in the remaining milk and the nutmeg. Add to the soup, return to the bowl, cover and cook on HIGH for 5 minutes.
5. Serve with a swirl of cream on each portion of soup.

CORN AND CHICKEN CHOWDER ✓

2 tablespoons butter	12 oz can whole kernel
1 onion, chopped	corn, drained
2 medium-size potatos	6 oz can evaporated milk
diced	1¼ cups cooked diced
2 tablespoons all-purpose	chicken
flour	salt and pepper to taste
¼ teaspoon turmeric	chopped parsley to garnish
2½ cups hot chicken stock	

1. Place the butter in a bowl and microwave on HIGH for 1 minute. Add the onion and potato and cook for 3 minutes.
2. Stir in the flour and turmeric, then blend in the chicken stock. Add two thirds of the corn, cover and cook on HIGH for 15 minutes.
3. Stir in the evaporated milk, then pour the soup into a blender or food processor; work until almost smooth.
4. Return to the bowl, add the chicken, reserved corn, and salt and pepper. Cover and cook on HIGH for 3 minutes. Serve garnished with chopped parsley.

Serves 4
Preparation time:
10 minutes
Power setting:
HIGH
Cooking time:
22 minutes

FRENCH-STYLE PATÉ

6–8 strips bacon
2 tablespoons butter
1/2 lb chicken livers,
chopped
1/2 lb ground pork
1/4 lb sausagemeat
1 clove garlic, crushed

3 tablespoons sherry
1 teaspoon chopped mixed
herbs
pinch of grated nutmeg
salt and pepper to taste
2–3 bay leaves

Serves 4–6
Preparation time:
15 minutes, plus
chilling time
Power setting:
HIGH
Cooking time:
10 minutes

1. Lay the bacon strips flat on a board and stretch with the back of a knife; use half to line a 7½ × 3½ × 2½ inch microwave loaf pan or earthenware terrine.
2. Combine the butter, livers, pork and sausagemeat in a bowl. Cover and cook on HIGH for 6 minutes or until the meat is cooked, stirring twice during cooking.
3. Place the mixture in a blender or food processor, add the garlic, sherry, herbs, nutmeg, and salt and pepper and work until smooth.
4. Spoon the mixture into the prepared pan and cover with the remaining bacon. Place 2 or 3 bay leaves on top. Cover with waxed paper and cook on HIGH for 4 minutes.
5. Leave to cool, then cover with foil, weight down and chill overnight.
6. Turn out onto a serving plate and slice. Serve with French bread and a green salad.

MINESTRONE

✓

A nourishing Italian vegetable soup, minestrone makes a hearty meal served with crisp rolls and butter. The vegetables used in this recipe can be varied, with the addition of cooked dried beans if you like.

1/4 cup olive oil
2 strips bacon, chopped
1 onion, chopped
1 clove garlic, crushed
2 celery sticks, sliced
2 carrots, diced
1 potato, diced
1/2 cup green beans
2 zucchini, diced

3 ripe tomatoes, skinned,
seeded and chopped
1 cup shredded Savoy
cabbage
1/4 cup tomato paste
1/4 cup small pasta shapes
4 cups hot chicken stock
salt and pepper to taste
freshly grated Parmesan
cheese to serve

1. Place the oil, bacon, onion, garlic and celery in a large bowl and cook on HIGH for 5 minutes.
2. Add the carrot and potato, cover and cook on HIGH for 5 minutes, stirring once or twice.
3. Cut the green beans into 1 inch lengths and add to the bowl with the zucchini. Cover and cook on HIGH for 2 minutes. Stir in the tomatoes, cabbage, tomato paste and pasta.
4. Add the hot chicken stock to the bowl, and season with salt and pepper. Cover the bowl and cook on HIGH for 10 minutes.
5. Serve in warmed individual soup bowls, with Parmesan cheese handed separately.

Serves 4–6
Preparation time: 15 minutes
Power setting: HIGH
Cooking time: 22 minutes

GINGER SHRIMP

✓

Serves 4
Preparation time:
10 minutes
Power setting:
HIGH
Cooking time:
2 minutes

¹/₂ lb medium-size shelled shrimp
1 cup bean sprouts
3 scallions, shredded
¹/₂ red pepper, sliced finely

1 teaspoon finely chopped fresh root ginger
2 teaspoons oyster sauce
2 teaspoons sesame oil
1 tablespoon soy sauce

Place all the ingredients in a large bowl, then cook on HIGH for 2 minutes. Stir and serve immediately.

MUSHROOM PATÉ

3 tablespoons butter
1 small onion, chopped
¹/₂ lb flat mushrooms

¹/₂ cup cream cheese
¹/₂ cup fresh breadcrumbs
salt and pepper to taste

Serves 4
Preparation time:
10 minutes, plus chilling time
Power setting:
HIGH
Cooking time:
6¹/₂ minutes

1. Place the butter in a bowl and microwave on HIGH for 30 seconds. Add the onion and cook for 2 minutes.
2. Chop the mushrooms finely, then squeeze them in paper towels to remove excess liquid. Add to the onion and cook on HIGH for 4 minutes. Drain well.
3. Transfer the mixture to a blender or food processor, add the remaining ingredients and work to a rough puree.
4. Spoon the paté into a serving dish, cover and chill for at least 4 hours or overnight. Serve with Melba toast.

DEVILED EARS OF CORN

¹/₃ cup butter
¹/₄ cup tomato catsup
2 teaspoons Worcestershire sauce

1 teaspoon Dijon mustard
4 ears of corn cobs

Serves 4
Preparation time:
5 minutes
Power setting:
HIGH
Cooking time:
12–15 minutes

1. Soften the butter in the microwave on HIGH for 30 seconds, then blend in the tomato catsup, Worcestershire sauce and mustard.
2. Place each ear of corn on a piece of waxed paper and spread with the butter mixture. Wrap the ears in the paper, and place in a large dish in a single layer.
3. Cook on HIGH until tender – about 12 minutes if fresh or 15 minutes if frozen; turn halfway through cooking.
4. Serve the corn with the buttery juices poured over.

CHICKEN TERIYAKI KEBABS

With its authentic Japanese flavor, this is a succulent and impressive way to serve chicken as an appetizer. To make scallion tassels for the garnish, trim the scallions and cut the green part into fine strips. Place in a bowl of ice water and leave to stand for about 30 minutes; drain on paper towels.

2 boneless chicken breasts, skinned
2 tablespoons soy sauce
1 teaspoon light brown granulated sugar, packed
2 tablespoons dry sherry

1 teaspoon finely chopped fresh root ginger
1 clove garlic, crushed
salad oil for brushing
TO GARNISH:
shredded lettuce
4 scallion tassels (see above)

Serves 4
Preparation time:
15 minutes, plus marinating
Power setting:
HIGH
Cooking time:
6 minutes

1. Cut the chicken into small pieces and place in a dish.
2. Combine the soy sauce, sugar, sherry, ginger and garlic, pour over the chicken and mix together. Cover and chill overnight.
3. Thread the chicken onto 8 wooden cocktail sticks. Place on a microwave rack over a dish, brush with oil and cook on HIGH for 6 minutes, turning halfway through cooking.
4. Serve hot, on a bed of shredded lettuce, garnished with the scallion tassels.

SHRIMP PROVENCALE

√

4 medium-size ripe tomatoes, skinned, seeded and chopped
1 tablespoon olive oil
1 small onion, chopped finely
1 clove garlic, crushed
1 teaspoon chopped basil

1 tablespoon tomato paste
1/2 lb medium-size shelled shrimp
1 tablespoon chopped red pepper
salt and pepper to taste
basil leaves to garnish

Serves 4
Preparation time:
10 minutes
Power setting:
HIGH
Cooking time:
13 minutes

1. Place the tomato flesh in a bowl with the oil, onion, garlic, basil, and salt and pepper. Cover and cook on HIGH for 10 minutes, stirring twice during cooking.
2. Place in a blender or food processor and work until smooth. Return to the bowl, stir in the remaining ingredients, cover and cook on HIGH for 3 minutes.
3. Spoon into individual dishes and garnish with basil. Serve with crusty French bread.

STILTON MUSHROOMS

¹/₂ lb large flat mushrooms
¹/₄ cup butter
¹/₂ cup chopped onion

6 oz Stilton or Danish Blue
*   cheese*
¹/₂ cup fresh breadcrumbs
salt and pepper to taste

1. Carefully remove the stalks from the mushrooms and chop finely. Wipe the caps with damp paper towels.
2. Place half of the butter in a bowl and microwave on HIGH for 1 minute, then add the mushroom stalks and onion and cook on HIGH for 2 minutes.
3. Leave to cool for 5 minutes, then crumble in the cheese, add the breadcrumbs, and salt and pepper and mix well. Divide the mixture between the mushroom caps.
4. Place the remaining butter in a large shallow dish and microwave on HIGH for 1 minute. Place the stuffed mushrooms in the dish and cook for 2 minutes.
5. Serve immediately.

Serves 4
Preparation time:
15 minutes
Power setting:
HIGH
Cooking time:
6 minutes

AVOCADO AND CRAB THERMIDOR

1 tablespoon butter
2 tablespoons all-purpose
* flour*
²/₃ cup milk
1 teaspoon tomato paste
juice of ¹/₂ lemon
good pinch of ground red
* pepper*

¹/₂ lb crabmeat, fresh,
* frozen or canned*
2 large avocados, halved
* and pitted*
4 teaspoons grated
* Parmesan cheese*
salt and pepper to taste

Serves 4
Preparation time:
10 minutes
Power setting:
HIGH
Cooking time:
7 minutes

1. Place the butter in a small bowl and microwave on HIGH for 30 seconds. Stir in the flour and return to the microwave for 30 seconds.
2. Pour the milk into a jug and heat on HIGH for 1 minute, then gradually blend into the butter and flour. Cook on HIGH for 2 minutes, whisking every 30 seconds.
3. Add the tomato paste, 1 teaspoon of the lemon juice, ground red pepper, and salt and pepper to the sauce, then stir in the crabmeat.
4. Sprinkle the avocado flesh with remaining lemon juice.
5. Pile the crabmeat filling into the avocado halves, then sprinkle with the Parmesan cheese. Place in a shallow dish and cook on HIGH for 3 minutes. Serve hot, with brown bread and butter.

HOT ANCHOVY DIP

This Italian dish, known as *Bagna Cauda*, is served as a hot dip for raw vegetables. It is ideal as a first course for a dinner party. If a small spirit burner is available, place the dip in a fondue dish over the burner to keep hot.

¹/₄ cup butter
¹/₄ cup olive oil
2 cloves garlic, chopped
2 oz can anchovies,
* drained*

TO SERVE:
variety of vegetables (e.g.
* celery, carrot, cucumber,*
* green or red pepper), cut*
* into strips*

Serves 4
Preparation time:
10 minutes
Power setting:
HIGH and
MEDIUM
Cooking time:
5 minutes

1. Place the butter and oil in a bowl and microwave on HIGH for 2 minutes. Add the garlic and cook for 1 minute.
2. Chop the anchovies, add them to the bowl, cover and cook on MEDIUM for 2 minutes.
3. Carefully transfer the mixture to a blender or food processor and work until smooth. Pour the dip into a warmed serving bowl, place on a large plate and surround with the vegetables. Serve immediately.

FLOUNDER ROLLS WITH CAPER SAUCE

√

8 flounder fillets, skinned
¼ cup dry white wine
1 tablespoon lemon juice
2 egg yolks

⅓ cup heavy cream
2 teaspoons capers
salt and pepper to taste

Serves 4
Preparation time:
15 minutes
Power setting:
HIGH
Cooking time:
7½ minutes

1. Roll up the flounder fillets and arrange in a shallow dish in a single layer. Mix together the wine and lemon juice, season with salt and pepper, then sprinkle over the fish. Cover and cook on HIGH for 5 minutes.
2. Using a slotted spoon, transfer the flounder rolls to a warmed serving dish and cover with foil to keep warm. Reserve the fish liquor.
3. Beat the egg yolks and cream together in a small bowl, then stir into the fish liquor. Add the capers, then cook on HIGH for 2½ minutes, stirring every 30 seconds.
4. Pour the sauce over the fish and serve immediately.

SPANISH FISH PARCELS

1½ lb coley, cod or
  haddock fillet, cut into 4
  pieces
1 tablespoon olive oil
½ each red and green
  pepper, cored, seeded
  and chopped
4 scallions, chopped

2 large tomatoes, skinned,
  seeded and chopped
2 celery sticks, chopped
1 clove garlic, crushed
salt and pepper to taste
flat-leaved parsley to
  garnish

Serves 4
Preparation time:
20 minutes
Power setting:
HIGH
Cooking time:
10 minutes

1. Place each piece of fish on a large piece of waxed paper.
2. Mix the remaining ingredients together in a bowl, cover and cook on HIGH for 3 minutes. Divide between the fish.
3. Wrap each piece of fish in its paper to make a parcel. Place in a dish and cook on HIGH for 7 minutes.
4. Unwrap each parcel and carefully lift the fish onto a warmed serving plate. Spoon the vegetables on top. Garnish with flat-leaved parsley to serve.

SRI LANKAN FISH

This quick curry is easy to prepare. The coconut and pineapple lend a delicate flavor to the fish and the subtle blend of spices gives a truly authentic taste.

1 onion, sliced
1½ lb thick haddock or
  cod fillet, skinned and
  cut into 3 inch pieces
3 dried red chilies, soaked
  for 10 minutes
½ cup unsweetened flaked
  coconut, blended with 1
  cup hot milk
½ teaspoon ground cumin
½ teaspoon turmeric
½ teaspoon ground
  fenugreek
pinch of ground cinnamon

1 tablespoon ground
  coriander
1 teaspoon finely grated
  fresh root ginger
1 teaspoon finely grated
  lemon rind
2 tablespoons lemon juice
8 oz can pineapple pieces
  in natural juice
1 tablespoon cornstarch,
  blended with 2
  tablespoons milk
salt and pepper to taste

Serves 4
Preparation time:
20 minutes
Power setting:
HIGH
Cooking time:
11 minutes

1. Place the onion in a large shallow dish, cover and cook on HIGH for 2 minutes. Lay the fish on top.
2. Seed and chop the chilies, then sprinkle over the fish.
3. Place the coconut milk, spices, grated ginger, and lemon rind and juice in a blender or food processor. Add the pineapple and its juice and work until smooth. Season with salt and pepper, then pour over the fish.
4. Cover and cook on HIGH for 6 minutes.
5. Stir in the blended cornstarch, being careful not to break up the fish, and cook on HIGH for 3 minutes or until the sauce thickens. Serve with boiled rice.

STUFFED COD STEAKS

4 cod cutlets, each about
  1 inch thick
2 tablespoons butter
1 small onion, chopped
1 cup fresh breadcrumbs
1 tablespoon chopped
  parsley
pinch of dried mixed herbs

1 tablespoon grated
  Parmesan cheese
2 tablespoons milk
salt and pepper to taste
2 tablespoons lemon juice
lemon wedges sprinkled
  with parsley to garnish

1. Cut away the center bone from each cod cutlet, then arrange the cutlets in a microwave dish.
2. Place the butter in a bowl and microwave on HIGH for 30 seconds. Add the onion and cook for 2 minutes. Stir in the breadcrumbs, parsley, dried herbs, Parmesan cheese, and salt and pepper, then add the milk to bind the stuffing together.
3. Spoon the stuffing into the eye of the cutlets, sprinkle with lemon juice, cover and cook on HIGH for 6 minutes.
4. Garnish with lemon wedges to serve.

Serves 4
Preparation time: 20 minutes
Power setting: HIGH
Cooking time: 8½ minutes

SPICED RICE CHICKEN

2 tablespoons butter
1 tablespoon salad oil
3/4 lb boneless skinned
    chicken breasts
1 onion, chopped
1 clove garlic, crushed
1 teaspoon each ground
    cumin and coriander

1/2 teaspoon ground ginger
1/2 teaspoon turmeric
1/2 cup orange juice
1 1/2 cups hot chicken stock
1 cup long-grain rice
1/3 cup golden raisins
salt and pepper to taste
cilantro leaves to garnish

Serves 4
Preparation time:
10 minutes
Power setting:
HIGH
Cooking time:
21 minutes
Standing time:
5 minutes

1. Place the butter and oil in a large bowl and microwave on HIGH for 1 minute. Cut the chicken into small pieces and add to the bowl with the onion and garlic. Cover and cook on HIGH for 5 minutes.
2. Stir in the spices, orange juice, stock and rice, season with salt and pepper, then cover and cook on HIGH for 15 minutes.
3. Add the golden raisins, then leave to stand for 5 minutes. Garnish with cilantro and serve with a cucumber salad.

CHICKEN LIVERS WITH SAGE

1/4 cup butter
1 onion, sliced
1 clove garlic, crushed
1/4 cup all-purpose flour
1 lb chicken livers
1/2 lb mushrooms, sliced

1 tablespoon dry white
    wine
2/3 cup sour cream
1 tablespoon chopped sage
salt and pepper to taste
sage leaves to garnish

Serves 4
Preparation time:
10 minutes
Power setting:
HIGH
Cooking time:
12 minutes

1. Place the butter in a large shallow dish and microwave on HIGH for 1 minute. Add the onion and garlic, cover and cook for 3 minutes.
2. Season the flour with salt and pepper and use to coat the chicken livers. Add to the dish, stir and cook on HIGH for 2 minutes.
3. Add the mushrooms, cover and cook on HIGH for 3 minutes. Stir in the wine and sour cream, add the sage, and salt and pepper and stir gently to mix. Cook on HIGH for 3 minutes.
4. Garnish with sage leaves and serve immediately with creamed potatoes or pasta and a green vegetable.

BOBOTIE

2 tablespoons butter
1 tablespoon salad oil
2 onions, chopped
1 clove garlic, crushed
3 teaspoons curry powder
1½ lb ground beef
⅓ cup golden raisins
1 tablespoon chutney

½ cup fresh breadcrumbs
2 eggs
⅔ cup milk
¼ cup slivered almonds,
   toasted
3 bay leaves
salt and pepper to taste

Serves 4
Preparation time:
10 minutes
Power setting:
HIGH
Cooking time:
25 minutes
Standing time:
5 minutes

1. Place the butter and oil in a large bowl and microwave on HIGH for 1 minute. Add the onions and garlic, cover and cook for 2 minutes. Stir in the curry powder and cook on HIGH for 2 minutes.
2. Mix in the ground beef and cook on HIGH for 5 minutes. Add the golden raisins, chutney, breadcrumbs, 1 egg, and pepper and mix well. Turn into a microwave serving dish.
3. Beat the remaining egg and milk together, pour over the meat, then sprinkle with the almonds. Place the bay leaves on top, then cook on HIGH for 15 minutes. Leave to stand, covered, for 5 minutes.

LEMON CHICKEN

1 tablespoon salad oil
1 lb boneless skinned
   chicken breasts, cut into
   thin strips
4 small zucchini, sliced
   thinly
1 cup thinly sliced carrot

1 teaspoon grated fresh
   root ginger
shredded rind of 1 lemon
5 scallions, chopped
2 tablespoons dry sherry
2 tablespoons soy sauce
juice of ½ lemon
2 teaspoons cornstarch

Serves 4
Preparation time:
15 minutes
Power setting:
HIGH
Cooking time:
12 minutes

1. Place the oil in a bowl and microwave on HIGH for 1 minute, add the chicken and cook on HIGH for 2 minutes.
2. Add the zucchini, carrot and ginger and cook on HIGH for 3 minutes.
3. Stir in the lemon rind, scallions, sherry and soy sauce, cover and cook on HIGH for 3 minutes.
4. Blend the lemon juice and cornstarch together, stir into the dish, cover and cook on HIGH for 3 minutes, until the sauce thickens.
5. Serve with boiled rice and shrimp crackers.

√

MEXICAN MEATBALLS

4 slices bread, crusts
    removed
1 lb ground beef
1 small onion, chopped
    finely
1 clove garlic, crushed
1 tablespoon chopped
    parsley
1/2 teaspoon ground red
    pepper, or to taste
1/2 teaspoon ground cumin
FOR THE SAUCE:
1 tablespoon salad oil
1 small onion, chopped
    finely

1 green pepper, cored,
    seeded and chopped
1 tablespoon all-purpose
    flour
1 1/4 cups tomato juice
1 tablespoon tomato paste
1 beef bouillon cube,
    blended with 1/4 cup
    boiling water
1 teaspoon chili sauce
1 teaspoon chopped
    oregano
15 oz can red kidney
    beans, drained
salt and pepper to taste

Serves 4
Preparation time:
20 minutes
Power setting:
HIGH
Cooking time:
14 minutes

1. Soak the bread in water to cover for 5 minutes, then squeeze dry and mash. Add the remaining ingredients with salt and pepper, and mix well.
2. Divide the mixture into 16 balls. Arrange in a single layer in a shallow dish and cook on HIGH for 5 minutes.
3. To make the sauce, put the oil and onion in a large shallow dish, cover and cook on HIGH for 2 minutes. Add the green pepper and cook for 1 minute.
4. Stir in the flour, then blend in the tomato juice and tomato paste. Add the remaining ingredients, with salt and pepper. Cover and cook on HIGH for 3 minutes.
5. Add the meatballs and their juices to the sauce and cook on HIGH for 3 minutes.
6. Serve with boiled rice and green salad.

BEEF AND OLIVE CASSEROLE

√

2 tablespoons olive oil
1 large onion, sliced
1 clove garlic, crushed
1 1/2 lb braising steak, cut
    into 2 inch cubes
1 1/4 cups red wine
1 beef bouillon cube
2/3 cup boiling water
2 long strips pared orange
    zest

1 bouquet garni
1/4 lb pitted black olives
1/4 lb mushrooms,
    quartered
2 tablespoons butter
1 tablespoon all-purpose
    flour
salt and pepper to taste

1. Place the oil, onion and garlic in a bowl and cook on HIGH for 3 minutes.

2. Add the steak, wine, crumbled bouillon cube, water, orange zest and bouquet garni and stir well. Cover and cook on HIGH for 10 minutes. Stir again, then cover and cook on LOW for 20 minutes.

3. Stir in the olives and mushrooms, cover and cook on LOW for 20 minutes. Remove the orange zest and bouquet garni.

4. Blend the butter and flour together to make a *beurre manié* paste, then stir into the casserole. Cover and cook on LOW for 10 minutes.

5. Leave to stand for 5–10 minutes. Serve with boiled rice.

Serves 4
Preparation time: 15 minutes
Power setting: HIGH and LOW
Cooking time: 1 hour 3 minutes
Standing time: 5–10 minutes

SAUSAGE COBBLER

Children will love the biscuit topping of this dish. The leeks could be changed to any vegetable of your choice, such as cauliflower, carrots or a can of white kidney beans.

1 lb thick pork sausages
1 tablespoon salad oil
1¹/₂ cups sliced leeks
3 tablespoons butter
¹/₃ cup all-purpose flour
2 cups milk
1 teaspoon chopped mixed herbs
salt and pepper to taste

FOR THE BISCUIT TOPPING:
2 cups whole wheat flour
2¹/₂ teaspoons baking powder
1 teaspoon dry mustard
¹/₄ cup margarine
¹/₂ cup grated Cheddar cheese
1 egg
about ¹/₄ cup milk

Serves 4
Preparation time:
25 minutes
Power setting:
HIGH
Cooking time:
21 minutes

1. Prick the sausages, place in a large shallow dish with the oil and cook on HIGH for 4 minutes, turning once. Drain on paper towels, discarding the oil and any fat. Leave to cool, then cut each sausage into 3 pieces.
2. Place the leeks in the dish with ¼ cup water, cover and cook on HIGH for 5 minutes. Drain and set aside.
3. Place the butter in a bowl and microwave on HIGH for 1 minute. Stir in the flour, then gradually blend in the milk. Cook on HIGH for 4 minutes, stirring twice. Add the herbs, and salt and pepper.
4. Add the leeks and sausages to the white sauce, then spoon into a round dish.
5. To make the biscuit topping, mix together the flour, baking powder, mustard and a pinch of salt. Rub in the margarine, then stir in the cheese.
6. Beat the egg and milk together. Set aside 1 tablespoon, then mix the rest into the rubbed-in mixture to make a soft dough.
7. Roll out the dough on a floured surface to a ½ inch thickness, then cut into rounds using a 2 inch plain cutter.
8. Lay the biscuits, slightly overlapping, on top of the sausage mixture, around the edge of the dish. Brush the biscuits with the reserved egg and milk mixture. Cook on HIGH for 7 minutes. Serve immediately.

ORANGE PORK CHOPS

4 pork chops
2 tablespoons butter
juice of 1 orange
1 tablespoon orange
  marmalade
2 rosemary sprigs, divided
  into pieces

1 teaspoon cornstarch,
  blended with 1
  tablespoon water
salt and pepper to taste
orange wedges to garnish

1. Sprinkle the chops with salt and pepper. Preheat a microwave browning skillet for 8 minutes, then allow the butter to melt on it. Place the chops on the hot skillet and cook on HIGH for 3 minutes. Turn the chops and cook on HIGH for 2 minutes.

2. Add the orange juice, marmalade and rosemary. Cover and cook on HIGH for 4 minutes.

3. Transfer the chops to a warmed serving dish, cover with foil and leave to stand for 2 minutes.

4. Meanwhile, add the orange juices from the skillet to the blended cornstarch, then cook on HIGH for 2 minutes.

5. Pour over the chops and garnish with orange to serve.

Serves 4
Preparation time:
20 minutes
Power setting:
HIGH
Cooking time:
11 minutes
Standing time:
2 minutes

MEDITERRANEAN LAMB

A succulent way of cooking a shoulder of lamb. Boning makes carving so much easier and the stuffing adds extra flavors to the meat. Serve for a special family meal.

1 tablespoon olive oil	*1 shoulder of lamb,*
1 small onion, chopped	*weighing 3¹/₂–4¹/₂ lb,*
finely	*boned*
1 clove garlic crushed	*²/₃ cup dry white wine*
³/₄ cup finely chopped	*1 teaspoon paprika*
mushrooms	*2 tablespoons tomato paste*
¹/₂ cup risotto rice, cooked	*1 each green, red and*
12 stuffed olives, chopped	*yellow pepper, cored*
finely	*and seeded*
1 teaspoon chopped	*1 tablespoon cornstarch,*
oregano	*blended with 2*
1 tablespoon chopped	*tablespoons water*
parsley	*salt and pepper to taste*

Serves 6–8
Preparation time:
30 minutes, plus
cooking rice
Power setting:
HIGH and
MEDIUM
Cooking time:
48 minutes–
1 hour,
approximately
Standing time:
25 minutes

1. Place the oil, onion and garlic in a small bowl, cover and cook on HIGH for 2 minutes. Add the mushrooms and cook for 1 minute. Stir in the rice, olives, herbs, and salt and pepper.
2. Place the lamb skin side down on a board and season well. Spread the rice mixture over the meat, roll up and tie securely with string. Weigh the joint and calculate the cooking time, allowing 12 minutes per lb on MEDIUM.
3. Place the lamb in a roasting bag in a dish and cook on MEDIUM for half of the calculated cooking time. Remove from the bag and place in the dish.
4. Mix the wine, paprika and tomato paste together, then pour over the lamb.
5. Cut the peppers into strips or chunks, then place around the lamb. Cover and cook on MEDIUM for the remaining cooking time.
6. Pour off the juices into a jug. Cover the lamb and peppers and leave to stand for 25 minutes.
7. Skim off the fat from the juices, add the blended cornstarch and cook on HIGH for 3 minutes. Stir in the peppers and season with salt and pepper if necessary.
8. Serve the lamb carved in slices with the sauce served separately.

MIDDLE EASTERN LAMB KEBABS

*1¹/₂ lb boneless leg of lamb
or neck fillet, cut into 1
inch cubes
¹/₂ cup dried apricots,
soaked overnight
FOR THE MARINADE:
¹/₄ cup olive oil
1 tablespoon wine vinegar*

*1 teaspoon ground cumin
1 small onion, chopped
finely
1 clove garlic, chopped
finely
1 tablespoon finely
chopped parsley
salt and pepper to taste*

1. Combine the marinade ingredients together in a bowl. Add the lamb, tossing to make sure each piece is covered. Cover and chill for about 8 hours, stirring occasionally.
2. Thread the lamb and apricots alternately on 4 wooden or bamboo skewers and arrange on a microwave roasting rack or large dish. Cover with waxed paper and cook on MEDIUM for 10 minutes.
3. Serve with plain boiled rice and a salad.

Serves 4
Preparation time:
15 minutes, plus
marinating
Power setting:
MEDIUM
Cooking time:
10 minutes

VEGETABLE DISHES

POTATO CAKE

This dish could be made into a substantial snack by adding chopped ham or salami.

1 cup grated potato
1 small onion, grated
1 tablespoon chopped parsley

2 tablespoons butter
salt and pepper to taste

Serves 2
Preparation time:
18 minutes
Power setting:
HIGH
Cooking time:
10 minutes

1. Preheat a browning skillet on HIGH for 8 minutes.
2. Meanwhile, mix together the potato, onion, parsley, and salt and pepper.
3. Place the butter on the hot skillet and microwave on HIGH for 1 minute. Quickly add the potato mixture, patting it down to a round shape with a fork. Cook on HIGH for 4 minutes.
4. Invert the potato cake onto a flat baking sheet, then slide it straight back onto the skillet. Cook for 5 minutes. Serve immediately.

SESAME CARROTS

Sesame seeds not only give the carrots a crunchy texture, but they are also rich in calcium and have a nutty flavor.

2¹/₂ cups thinly sliced carrots
1 tablespoon sesame seeds

2 tablespoons butter
salt and pepper to taste

Serves 4
Preparation time:
10 minutes
Power setting:
HIGH
Cooking time:
12 minutes
Standing time:
2 minutes

1. Place the carrots and ¼ cup water in a dish, cover and cook on HIGH for 8 minutes, stirring halfway through cooking. Leave to stand for 2 minutes.
2. Put the sesame seeds in a shallow container and cook on HIGH for 2 minutes. Set aside.
3. Drain the carrots, add the butter and cook on HIGH for 2 minutes. Season with salt and pepper and toss well.
4. Spoon into a warmed serving dish and sprinkle with the sesame seeds to serve.

CARROT AND CHEESE RING

This vegetable dish would made a good accompaniment to a vegetarian meal. It is also delicious cold.

5 cups grated carrots	*1 egg, beaten*
3 scallions, chopped finely	*2 tablespoons chopped*
1/2 cup grated Cheddar	*parsley*
cheese	*salt and pepper to taste*
3 tablespoons milk	*watercress sprigs to garnish*

Serves 6
Preparation time:
15 minutes
Power setting:
HIGH
Cooking time:
13 minutes

1. Place the carrots in a bowl, cover and cook on HIGH for 5 minutes.
2. Add the remaining ingredients, then spoon into a greased 5 cup ring mold, pressing evenly.
3. Cover with waxed paper and cook on HIGH for 8 minutes. Turn onto a plate and garnish with watercress.

STUFFED ZUCCHINI

Zucchini with a savory filling make a delicious appetizer, vegetarian meal or accompaniment to fish or chicken.

4 zucchini, halved	*1/2 cup medium oatmeal*
lengthways	*pinch of ground red pepper*
1 small onion, chopped	*1/2 cup grated Cheddar*
2 tomatoes, skinned,	*cheese*
seeded and chopped	*salt and pepper to taste*
1 cup cottage cheese	*flat-leaved parsley to*
1 tablespoon chopped	*garnish*
parsley	

Serves 4 as an
appetizer,
Serves 2 as a main
meal
Preparation time:
20 minutes
Power setting:
HIGH
Cooking time:
12 minutes
Standing time:
2 minutes

1. Using a teaspoon, scoop out the centers from the zucchini halves. Sprinkle the insides of the zucchini shells with salt and pepper and set aside.
2. Chop the zucchini flesh and place in a bowl with the onion. Cover and cook on HIGH for 3 minutes.
3. Stir in the tomatoes, cottage cheese, parsley, oatmeal, ground red pepper and salt and pepper.
4. Wipe off the moisture inside the zucchini shells with paper towels, then fill with the stuffing mixture. Place in a dish and sprinkle with the grated cheese.
5. Cook on HIGH for 9 minutes. Leave to stand for 2 minutes. Garnish with parsley to serve.

CORIANDER MUSHROOMS

2 tablespoons olive oil
2 cloves garlic, crushed
1 lb large mushrooms,
  sliced thickly
1 teaspoon coriander
  seeds, crushed

3 tablespoons Greek
  strained yogurt (cow's)
salt and pepper to taste
chopped parsley to garnish

1. Place the oil and garlic in a large shallow dish and cook on HIGH for 2 minutes. Stir in the mushrooms, making sure they are all coated with the oil, and cook for 3 minutes, stirring them halfway through cooking.
2. Mix in the coriander seeds, yogurt, and salt and pepper and cook on HIGH for 1 minute. Sprinkle with parsley and serve immediately.

Serves 4
Preparation time:
10 minutes
Power setting:
HIGH
Cooking time:
6 minutes

LENTIL CURRY

Serve as an accompaniment to a meat or chicken curry, or as a main course for a vegetarian meal.

1 onion, chopped
2 tablespoons salad oil
2 teaspoons hot curry
*   powder*
1 cup red lentils

3 cups hot vegetable stock
2 tablespoons mango
*   chutney*
salt and pepper to taste

Serves 4–6
Preparation time:
10 minutes
Power setting:
HIGH
Cooking time:
23 minutes

1. Place the onion and oil in a bowl, cover and cook on HIGH for 2 minutes. Add the curry powder and cook for 1 minute.
2. Stir in the remaining ingredients, cover and cook on HIGH for 20 minutes. Check the seasoning, stir well then transfer to a warmed serving dish.

EGGPLANT LAYER

1 medium-size eggplant,
*   cut into ¼ inch slices*
1 onion, chopped
2 tablespoons salad oil
1 clove garlic, crushed
½ lb mushrooms, chopped
3 medium-size tomatoes,
*   skinned and chopped*

2 teaspoons tomato paste
1 teaspoon dried oregano
3 oz lasagna, cooked
⅔ cup plain yogurt
1 egg, beaten
2 teaspoons grated
*   Parmesan cheese*
salt and pepper to taste

Serves 4–6
Preparation time:
25 minutes, plus
standing time
Power setting:
HIGH
Cooking time:
32 minutes
Standing time:
5 minutes

1. Sprinkle the eggplant slices with salt, place in a colander and leave to stand for 1 hour. Rinse well, pat dry on paper towels, then place in a bowl, cover and cook on HIGH for 4 minutes. Set aside.
2. Place the onion and oil in another bowl and cook on HIGH for 3 minutes. Add the garlic, mushrooms, tomatoes, tomato paste, oregano, and salt and pepper, cover and cook on HIGH for 5 minutes.
3. Arrange a third of the lasagna in a shallow dish, cover with a third of the tomato sauce, and finish with a third of the eggplant slices. Repeat these layers twice.
4. Beat the yogurt and egg together, season with salt and pepper, then spoon over the eggplant. Sprinkle with the Parmesan and cook on HIGH for 20 minutes.
5. Leave to stand for 5 minutes. Serve with salad.

TOMATO AND POTATO BAKE

3/4 lb potatoes, sliced thinly
1 large onion, sliced
3 tablespoons butter
4 medium-size tomatoes,
  skinned and sliced

1/4 cup whipping cream
1/2 teaspoon chopped basil
salt and pepper to taste

Serves 4–6
Preparation time:
15 minutes
Power setting:
HIGH
Cooking time:
16 minutes

1. Place the potatoes in a large shallow dish with $\frac{1}{4}$ cup water. Place another fitting dish on top and put into it the onion and butter. Place the 2 dishes in the oven and cook on HIGH for 6 minutes, stirring the onion twice during cooking.
2. Arrange half of the potatoes in a serving dish. Cover with half of the tomatoes, then two thirds of the onion. Spoon over half of the cream and basil, then season with salt and pepper.
3. Repeat the potato and tomato layers, pile the remaining onion in the center and spoon the remaining cream over the tomatoes. Season with the remaining basil, and salt and pepper, then cook on HIGH for 10 minutes.
4. Serve with any roast meat.

STUFFED PEPPERS

These stuffed peppers make an ideal vegetarian meal. Serve with a leafy salad and whole grain bread.

4 large peppers
2 tablespoons salad oil
1 onion, chopped
3 celery sticks, chopped
1/4 lb mushrooms, chopped
2 cups whole wheat
  breadcrumbs

1/2 cup chopped Brazil nuts
1/2 teaspoon dried mixed
  herbs
1 cup grated Cheddar
  cheese
salt and pepper to taste

Serves 4
Preparation time:
15 minutes
Power setting:
HIGH
Cooking time:
15 minutes
Standing time:
2 minutes

1. Slice the tops off the peppers and remove the seeds.
2. Place the oil in a bowl with the onion, cover and cook on HIGH for 3 minutes. Add the celery and mushrooms and cook for 2 minutes.
3. Mix in the remaining ingredients, then spoon into the peppers. Replace the tops and stand the peppers upright close together in a dish.
4. Pour in $\frac{1}{4}$ cup water, cover and cook on HIGH for 10 minutes. Stand for 2 minutes before serving.

PRAIRIE POTATOES

✓

4 potatoes, each weighing
½ lb
2 tablespoons butter
¼ cup milk
½ lb corned beef, diced

7 oz can whole kernel
corn, drained
2 tablespoons chutney
1 cup grated Cheddar
cheese
salt and pepper to taste

Serves 4
Preparation time:
10 minutes
Power setting:
HIGH
Cooking time:
21 minutes
Standing time:
5 minutes

1. Prick the potato skins, wrap each one in a paper towel and cook on HIGH for 10 minutes. Turn the potatoes over and cook for 7 minutes. Leave to stand for 5 minutes.
2. Cut the potatoes in half and scoop out the flesh into a bowl. Add the butter and milk and mash well. Stir in the corned beef, corn, chutney, half of the cheese, and salt and pepper.
3. Spoon the filling into the potato skins and top with the remaining cheese. Cook on HIGH for 4 minutes. Serve immediately with a green salad.

DEVILED KIDNEY AND MUSHROOMS

12 lambs' kidneys
2 tablespoons butter
1 small onion, chopped
finely
½ lb mushrooms,
quartered
2 teaspoons Dijon mustard

1 tablespoon
Worcestershire sauce
2 teaspoons cornstarch
2 tablespoons whipping
cream
salt and pepper to taste
toast triangles to serve

Serves 4
Preparation time:
15 minutes
Power setting:
HIGH
Cooking time:
14 minutes

1. Cut the kidneys in half lengthways, remove the membranes and cores and set aside.
2. Place the butter in a shallow dish and microwave on HIGH for 1 minute. Add the onion; cook for 3 minutes.
3. Stir in the kidneys, cover and cook on HIGH for 2 minutes. Add the mushrooms and cook for 3 minutes.
4. Mix the mustard and Worcestershire sauce into the kidneys, stir, cover and cook on HIGH for 3 minutes.
5. Blend the cornstarch with the cream, stir into the kidney mixture, cover and cook on HIGH for 2 minutes. Season with salt and pepper. Serve with toast triangles.

SARDINE PIZZA

1 tablespoon salad oil
1 small onion, chopped
14 oz can chopped
    tomatoes
15 oz can sardines in
    tomato sauce, drained
pinch of dried mixed herbs
1/2 cup grated Cheddar
    cheese

salt and pepper to taste
FOR THE BASE:
2 cups self-rising flour
1 teaspoon baking powder
pinch of salt
1/4 cup margarine
1 egg, beaten
3 tablespoons milk

Serves 4
Preparation time:
15 minutes
Power setting:
HIGH
Cooking time:
9 minutes

1. Place the oil and onion in a small bowl and cook on HIGH for 2 minutes. Stir in the tomatoes, then set aside.
2. Make the pizza base: sift the flour, baking powder and salt into a bowl, then rub in the margarine until the mixture resembles breadcrumbs. Add the egg and milk and mix to a soft dough.
3. Knead lightly, then roll out on a floured surface to a 10 inch circle. Place on waxed paper, set on the microwave turntable or on a large flat plate and cook on HIGH for 4 minutes. Remove the paper and return the base to the turntable or plate.
4. Spread the tomatoes over the base. Split the sardines in half and remove any bones, then arrange on top of the tomatoes. Sprinkle with the herbs, salt and pepper, then the grated cheese. Cook the pizza on HIGH for 3 minutes.
5. Serve immediately, with a mixed green salad.

VARIATION
Replace the sardines with flaked tuna fish. Add a few anchovies, if liked, arranged in a lattice pattern over the top of the cheese.

FISHERMAN'S PIE

1 1/2 lb potatoes, sliced
    thinly
2 cups frozen mixed
    vegetables
2 × 7 oz cans tuna in
    brine, drained
2 oz package onion sauce
    mix

1 1/4 cups milk
2 hard-boiled eggs,
    chopped
2 tablespoons butter
1 tablespoon finely
    chopped parsley
salt and pepper to taste

1. Place the potatoes in a dish with ½ cup water. Cover and cook on HIGH for 9 minutes. Leave to stand for 5 minutes, then drain.
2. Meanwhile, place the mixed vegetables in a bowl, add ¼ cup water, cover and cook on HIGH for 5 minutes. Drain, then return to the bowl.
3. Add the tuna to the vegetables and stir together to break up the tuna chunks a little.
4. Place the onion sauce mix in a jug, stir in the milk, then cook on HIGH for 4 minutes, stirring twice during cooking.
5. Pour the sauce over the tuna and vegetables, add the chopped eggs, and salt and pepper, then spoon into a dish.
6. Add the butter to the potatoes and mash well. Season with salt and pepper, add the parsley and beat thoroughly.
7. Put the potato mixture into a piping bag fitted with a large nozzle and pipe a border around the edge of the dish. Alternatively, spread the potato over the top and mark the surface with a fork. Cook on HIGH for 5 minutes.

Serves 4
Preparation time:
20 minutes
Power setting:
HIGH
Cooking time:
23 minutes
Standing time:
5 minutes

BROCCOLI AND HAM IN CHEESE SAUCE

8 broccoli spears
2 tablespoons butter
¼ cup all-purpose flour
2 cups milk
1 teaspoon mustard

¼ teaspoon ground red
*   pepper*
1 cup grated Cheddar
*   cheese*
8 thin slices ham
salt to taste

Serves 4
Preparation time:
10 minutes
Power setting:
HIGH
Cooking time:
16 minutes

1. Arrange the broccoli in a large shallow dish, with the heads in the center and the stalks radiating out to the sides. Add ¼ cup boiling water, cover and cook on HIGH for 8 minutes. Drain and set aside.
2. Place the butter in a bowl and microwave on HIGH for 1 minute. Stir in the flour and microwave for 30 seconds. Gradually stir in the milk, then cook on HIGH for 4 minutes, stirring twice during cooking.
3. Whisk the mustard and ground red pepper into the sauce, add the cheese and season with salt.
4. Wrap each broccoli spear in a slice of ham, arrange in a dish, then pour over the cheese sauce. Cook on HIGH for 3 minutes. Brown under a hot grill if you wish.
5. Serve immediately, with crusty bread and tomato salad.

MACARONI CHEESE WITH BACON

1¾ cups macaroni
⅓ lb bacon, chopped
2 tablespoons butter
3 tablespoons all-purpose
*   flour*

2½ cups milk
1 teaspoon mustard
1 cup grated Cheddar
*   cheese*
salt and pepper to taste

Serves 4
Preparation time:
15 minutes
Power setting:
HIGH
Cooking time:
25 minutes

1. Place the macaroni in a large bowl with 5 cups boiling water and a pinch of salt. Cover and cook on HIGH for 10 minutes; drain and keep warm.
2. Place the bacon and butter in a bowl, cover and cook on HIGH for 5 minutes. Stir in the flour, then gradually add the milk. Cook on HIGH, uncovered, for 4 minutes, stirring every minute.
3. Stir the mustard and three-quarters of the cheese into the sauce and season with salt and pepper. Fold the macaroni into the sauce, then pour into a casserole.
4. Sprinkle over the remaining cheese and cook, uncovered, on HIGH for 6 minutes.
5. Broil to brown if desired.

TAGLIATELLE WITH CHEESE AND NUTS

For those counting calories, substitute a low-fat cream cheese with herbs and garlic and serve with a green salad. For another variation, substitute chopped ham for the walnuts.

½ lb dried tagliatelle
1 tablespoon salad oil
2 tablespoons whipping
*   cream*

½ cup cream cheese with
*   herbs and garlic*
¾ cup chopped walnuts
salt and pepper to taste

Serves 4
Preparation time:
5 minutes
Power setting:
HIGH
Cooking time:
7½ minutes
Standing time:
3 minutes

1. Place the tagliatelle in a large bowl or wide shallow dish, add the oil and 1 teaspoon salt, then pour over 5 cups boiling water, making sure the noodles are covered. Cover and cook on HIGH for 6 minutes. Leave to stand for 3 minutes.
2. Drain the noodles, then return to the bowl. Stir in the cream, add the cheese in pieces, then the walnuts. Season with salt and pepper and toss together.
3. Cover and cook on HIGH for 1½ minutes, until the cheese melts.
4. Toss again, then divide between 4 individual dishes and serve immediately.

SPICY INDIAN OMELET

This is an unusual way of cooking an omelet. The result is much thicker and more solid than an ordinary omelet, therefore longer, slower cooking is required.

2 tablespoons butter
2 tablespoons cornstarch
²/₃ cup plain yogurt
8 eggs
1 small onion, chopped finely
1 tablespoon finely chopped parsley

½ teaspoon ground coriander
¼ teaspoon ground red pepper
¼ teaspoon turmeric
½ teaspoon cumin seeds, crushed
½ cup frozen peas, thawed
salt to taste

1. Place the butter in a large shallow dish and microwave on MEDIUM for 1 minute.
2. Blend the cornstarch and yogurt together, beat in the eggs, then add the remaining ingredients.
3. Pour the egg mixture into the dish and cook on MEDIUM for 5 minutes, drawing the edges of the omelet into the center every minute. Cook for a further 5 minutes on MEDIUM.
4. Leave to stand for 1 minute, then cut into wedges and serve with a tomato and cucumber salad and poppadoms.

Serves 4
Preparation time:
10 minutes
Power setting:
MEDIUM
Cooking time:
11 minutes
Standing time:
1 minute

PAELLA

Paella is Spain's most famous dish, the main ingredients being rice, olive oil and saffron. It can be simple, but for a special occasion, the addition of shellfish, spicy sausage and meat makes it very colorful and an ideal dish to serve for a buffet.

¼ cup olive oil
2 lb chicken, cut into 6 pieces
¼ lb pork fillet, cut into small cubes
1 onion, chopped finely
2 cloves garlic, chopped finely
1 red pepper, cored, seeded and cut into strips
1¾ cups long-grain rice
½ teaspoon paprika
pinch of powdered saffron (optional)

3½ cups boiling chicken stock
¼ lb chorizo or garlic sausage, sliced thinly
6 raw large shrimp (optional)
1 cup frozen peas, thawed
¼ lb medium-size shelled shrimp
8 oz can mussels in brine, drained
4 tomatoes, skinned, seeded and chopped
salt and pepper to taste

Serves 6
Preparation time: 30 minutes
Power setting: HIGH
Cooking time: 32 minutes
Standing time: 12 minutes

1. Pour the oil into a large dish and microwave on HIGH for 2 minutes. Add the chicken pieces, skin side down, cover and cook on HIGH for 5 minutes. Add the pork and cook for 3 minutes. Remove the meats with a slotted spoon and set aside.
2. Add the onion, garlic and red pepper to the bowl and cook on HIGH for 2 minutes. Stir in the rice and mix well, then add the paprika, saffron, if using, and stock. Return the meats to the bowl, cover and cook on HIGH for 15 minutes. Leave to stand for 10 minutes.
3. Stir in the sausage, large shrimp, if using, peas, shelled shrimp, mussels, tomatoes, and salt and pepper. Cover and cook on HIGH for 5 minutes. Leave to stand for 2 minutes before serving.

CHICKEN KORMA

This mild and creamy curry is traditionally served on special occasions in India. Accompany the dish with rice and poppadoms and hand round dishes of chutney, chopped onion and sliced tomato.

3¹/₂ lb chicken, cut into 8
pieces and skinned
²/₃ cup plain yogurt
2 cloves garlic, crushed
2 teaspoons turmeric
3 tablespoons butter
1 large onion, sliced
2 inch piece fresh root
ginger, peeled and cut
into thin strips
¹/₂ teaspoon ground red
pepper

1 teaspoon coriander
seeds, crushed
5 whole cloves
1 teaspoon salt
2 inch piece cinnamon
stick
2 teaspoons cornstarch
²/₃ cup whipping cream
¹/₄ cup unsalted cashew
nuts, browned (see page
7)

Serves 4
Preparation time:
20 minutes, plus marinating
Power setting:
HIGH and MEDIUM
Cooking time:
21 minutes
Standing time:
5 minutes

1. Place the chicken pieces in a dish. Mix together the yogurt, garlic and turmeric and pour over the chicken. Cover and leave to marinate overnight in the refrigerator.
2. Place the butter in a large casserole and microwave on HIGH for 1 minute. Add the onion and cook for 3 minutes.
3. Stir the ginger, ground red pepper and coriander into the onion and cook on HIGH for 1 minute.
4. Add the chicken with its marinade, the cloves, salt and cinnamon stick, cover and cook on HIGH for 7 minutes.
5. Stir and rearrange the chicken pieces, then cook on MEDIUM for 6 minutes.
6. Blend the cornstarch with the cream, stir into the chicken and cook on HIGH for 3 minutes. Leave to stand for 5 minutes. Sprinkle with the nuts to serve.

GAME HENS CHAMPENOISE

This delicious dinner party dish is made with inexpensive sparkling wine and garnished with grapes.

4 Rock Cornish game hens
¹/₃ cup butter
1¹/₄ cups dry sparkling
white wine
1 chicken bouillon cube

¹/₂ lb seedless grapes
2 tablespoons all-purpose
flour
salt and pepper to taste

1. Season the game hens inside and out with salt and pepper and put a knob of butter inside each body cavity.
2. Heat a browning skillet on HIGH for 8 minutes. Add 2 tablespoons of the remaining butter to the skillet and microwave on HIGH for 1 minute.
3. Place the game hens, breasts down, on the skillet and cook on HIGH for 2 minutes. Turn the birds over and cook for 2 minutes.
4. Transfer the game hens to a large casserole, pour over the wine and add the bouillon cube. Cover and cook on HIGH for 15 minutes.
5. Add the grapes and cook on HIGH for 5 minutes.
6. Remove the game hens with a slotted spoon and discard any trussing string. Place on a warmed serving dish.
7. Remove the grapes with a slotted spoon and arrange around the game hens. Cover with foil to keep warm.
8. Blend the remaining butter with the flour, whisk into the cooking liquid and cook on HIGH for 6 minutes, stirring twice, until thickened. Season with salt and pepper.
9. Pour a little sauce over the game hens and serve the remaining sauce separately.

Serves 4
Preparation time:
30 minutes
Power setting:
HIGH
Cooking time:
31 minutes

TARRAGON TROUT

¼ cup butter	*2 tablespoons dry white*
1 small onion, chopped	*wine*
½ lb mushrooms, chopped	*salt and pepper to taste*
1 tablespoon chopped	*TO GARNISH:*
tarragon	*lemon slices*
4 trout, cleaned	*tarragon sprigs*

Serves 4
Preparation time:
10 minutes
Power setting:
HIGH
Cooking time:
16 minutes

1. Place the butter in a bowl and microwave on HIGH for 1 minute. Add the onion and cook on HIGH for 1 minute. Stir in the mushrooms and cook for 2 minutes. Add the tarragon, and salt and pepper.
2. Make 2 slits on each side of each fish to prevent the skin from bursting during cooking. Divide the mushroom mixture between the trout, stuffing it into the body cavity. Shield the tails with foil.
3. Place the fish in a shallow dish, pour over the wine, cover and cook on HIGH for 12 minutes, changing the position of the fish halfway through cooking.
4. Garnish with the lemon slices and tarragon to serve.

SALMON WITH DILL SAUCE

4 salmon steaks, about 1	*½ cup butter*
inch thick	*1 tablespoon chopped dill*
¼ cup water	*salt and pepper to taste*
juice of ½ lemon	*dill sprigs to garnish*
2 egg yolks	

Serves 4
Preparation time:
10 minutes
Power setting:
HIGH
Cooking time:
8 minutes

1. Arrange the salmon in a large shallow dish. Mix the water with 1 tablespoon of the lemon juice, season with salt, then pour over the fish.
2. Cover with waxed paper and cook on HIGH for 6 minutes. Set aside while making the sauce.
3. Place the egg yolks in a blender or food processor and work for 30 seconds. Place the butter in a dish and microwave on HIGH for 1 minute, then add the remaining lemon juice.
4. With the motor running, pour the butter in a steady stream onto the egg yolks until combined. Pour into a bowl and stir in the chopped dill and salt and pepper.
5. Arrange the salmon on a warmed serving plate and spoon a little of the sauce over each portion. Garnish each with a sprig of dill.

SEAFOOD AND WATERCRESS SOUFFLÉ

This unusual dish has a layer of creamy fish and a layer of watercress soufflé—light in texture and rich in flavor. Use any combination of white fish: try monkfish and lemon sole for a special occasion and a few sliced scallops for extra luxury.

1 lb white fish, e.g.
  flounder fillets, lemon
  sole, skinned
2 tablespoons dry white
  wine
2 teaspoons cornstarch
¼ cup heavy cream
6 eggs, separated
¼ lb medium-size shelled
  shrimp
3 tablespoons butter
⅓ cup all-purpose flour

1¼ cups milk
¼ teaspoon ground mace
pinch of ground red pepper
2 bunches watercress,
  chopped finely
2 tablespoons grated
  Parmesan cheese
salt and pepper to taste
TO GARNISH:
watercress sprigs, medium-
  size unshelled shrimp

Serves 4
Preparation time:
25 minutes
Power setting:
HIGH
Cooking time:
18 minutes
Standing time:
2 minutes

1. Cut the fish into 1 inch pieces and place in a dish. Sprinkle with the wine, cover and cook on HIGH for 3 minutes. Drain thoroughly, reserving the liquor.
2. Blend together the cornstarch, cream and 1 egg yolk in a bowl, then gradually stir in the fish liquor. Cook on HIGH for 2 minutes, whisking every 30 seconds. Whisk again until smooth and season with salt and pepper.
3. Carefully fold the cooked fish and the shrimp into the sauce, then spoon into a greased 9 inch soufflé dish or microwave container.
4. Place the butter in a large bowl and microwave on HIGH for 1 minute. Beat in the flour, then gradually add the milk. Cook on HIGH for 2 minutes, stirring every 30 seconds, then give the sauce a good whisk until glossy. Season with the mace, ground red pepper, and salt and pepper.
5. Add the remaining egg yolks, beating well after each addition, then stir in the watercress and Parmesan cheese.
6. Whisk the egg whites until stiff, then carefully fold into the watercress mixture. Pour into the dish, covering the fish evenly and cook on HIGH for 10 minutes.
7. Leave to stand for 2 minutes; the soufflé will shrink away from the edge.
8. Carefully turn out onto a warmed serving plate and garnish with watercress and shrimp to serve.

VEAL CHOPS WITH RED PEPPER SAUCE

4 veal chops
microwave seasoning
1 small onion, chopped
2 red peppers, cored,
  seeded and chopped

1 clove garlic, chopped
²/₃ cup light stock
2 tablespoons salad oil
salt and pepper to taste
snipped chives to garnish

1. Sprinkle the chops with the microwave seasoning and set aside.
2. Place the onion in a bowl, cover and cook on HIGH for 2 minutes. Add the red pepper, garlic and stock, cover and cook on HIGH for 10 minutes. Leave to stand for 10 minutes.
3. Meanwhile, heat a browning skillet on HIGH for 8 minutes. Pour over the oil and heat for 2 minutes.
4. Place the veal chops on the skillet and cook on HIGH for 6 minutes on each side.
5. While they are cooking, place the red pepper mixture in a blender or food processor and work until smooth. Season with salt and pepper if necessary. Reheat the sauce on HIGH for 2 minutes just before serving.
6. Pour the red pepper sauce over the chops and garnish with chives. Serve with snow peas.

Serves 4
Preparation time:
30 minutes
Power setting:
HIGH
Cooking time:
24 minutes

SWEET AND SOUR PORK

8 oz can pineapple slices in
natural juice
2 tablespoons soy sauce
3 tablespoons orange juice
1 tablespoon lemon juice
2 tablespoons tomato
catsup
2 tablespoons olive oil

1 tablespoon honey
1 tablespoon grated fresh
root ginger
2 lb pork tenderloin, cut
into ¼ inch slices
2 tablespoons cornstarch
salt and pepper to taste

Serves 4–6
Preparation time:
10 minutes, plus
marinating
Power setting:
HIGH
Cooking time:
12 minutes

1. Drain the pineapple, reserving the juice, and cut the slices into quarters. Set aside.
2. Place the soy sauce, orange and lemon juice, catsup, oil, honey and ginger in a large bowl. Add half of the pineapple juice and mix well. Add the pork, toss well to coat in the marinade, cover and chill for 2 hours.
3. Cover the bowl and cook on HIGH for 5 minutes. Add the pineapple.
4. Blend the cornstarch with the remaining pineapple juice, stir into the pork, and season with salt and pepper. Cover and cook on HIGH for 7 minutes.
5. Serve with boiled rice or egg noodles.

PORK SATÉ

This Indonesian dish consists of marinated cubes of meat cooked on skewers and served with a spicy peanut sauce. For chicken saté, use 1 lb boneless chicken breast; for beef saté use 1 lb rump steak.

1¼ lb pork tenderloin, cut
into 1 inch cubes
½ teaspoon ground red
pepper
½ teaspoon turmeric
1 teaspoon ground
coriander
1 teaspoon ground cumin
½ teaspoon salt
2 tablespoons soy sauce
1 tablespoon salad oil
FOR THE SAUCE:
1 tablespoon salad oil

1 very small onion,
chopped finely
1 clove garlic, crushed
3 tablespoons peanut
butter
½ teaspoon ground red
pepper
1 teaspoon light brown
sugar
1 teaspoon lemon juice
TO GARNISH:
scallion tassels (see page
16)

1. Place the pork in a bowl, Mix together the spices, salt and soy sauce, then mix into the pork, using your hands to knead the spices into the meat. Cover and leave in a cool place to marinate for at least 6 hours.
2. Thread the pork cubes onto bamboo or wooden skewers, brush with the oil and place on a microwave roasting rack or large microwave dish, over a bowl. Cover with waxed paper and microwave on MEDIUM for 10 minutes, rearranging and turning the kebabs after 5 minutes. Wrap in foil and leave to stand for 5 minutes.
3. To make the sauce, mix the ingredients together in a bowl and cook on HIGH for 1 minute. Serve hot with the pork. Garnish the dish with scallion tassels.

Serves 4
Preparation time: 10 minutes, plus marinating
Power setting: HIGH and MEDIUM
Cooking time: 11 minutes
Standing time: 5 minutes

HAM WITH GREEN PEPPER SAUCE

Green peppercorns are pungent in flavor and add spiciness to a dish. They are available fresh, but you may wish to buy some preserved in brine for future use.

2–3 lb smoked ham joint,
soaked overnight
2 tablespoons butter
¼ cup all-purpose flour

⅔ cup whipping cream
1 tablespoon green
peppercorns

Serves 4–6
Preparation time:
10 minutes, plus
overnight soaking
Power setting:
HIGH and
MEDIUM
Cooking time:
27–39 minutes
Standing time:
20 minutes

1. Drain the ham joint and place in a roasting bag. Tie loosely with string and cook on MEDIUM, allowing 12 minutes per lb; turn the joint over halfway through cooking.
2. Snip a corner from the roasting bag and pour off the juices into a measuring jug. Skim off any fat from the surface and make up to ⅔ cup with water. Leave the joint to stand for 20 minutes.
3. Meanwhile, place the butter in a bowl and microwave on HIGH for 1 minute. Stir in the flour, then the ham juices and cream. Cook on HIGH for 2 minutes, stirring every 30 seconds. Add the peppercorns and keep warm.
4. Remove the rind from the joint and carve the meat into slices. Arrange on a warmed serving plate, pour over a little sauce and serve the remaining sauce separately.

LAMB IN RED WINE

Boning and rolling lamb is not too difficult but it is quicker and easier to buy ready-prepared noisettes.

2 lb best end of neck of
lamb, or 8 noisettes of
lamb, each 1 inch thick
1 cup red wine
1 clove garlic, crushed
few rosemary sprigs

1 tablespoon tomato paste
1 tablespoon butter
2 tablespoons all-purpose
flour
salt and pepper to taste
parsley sprigs to garnish

1. To prepare noisettes yourself, skin the best end of neck, then place fat side down on a board and cut the meat from the bones with a sharp knife. Season with salt and pepper, roll up tightly and tie at 1 inch intervals with fine string. Cut through the meat between the string to make noisettes. Place in a shallow bowl.

2. Mix the wine, garlic, rosemary, tomato paste, and salt and pepper together, then pour over the lamb. Cover and leave to marinate for 3 hours.

3. Cook on HIGH for 8 minutes. Remove lamb, return dish to oven and cook for 5 minutes. Discard the rosemary.

4. Meanwhile, remove string from the lamb and arrange on a warmed serving dish; cover with foil to keep warm.

5. Mash the butter and flour together with a fork, then whisk into the sauce. Cook on HIGH for 2 minutes.

6. Pour over the lamb and garnish with parsley. Serve with thin-skinned potatoes and a julienne of vegetables.

Serves 4
Preparation time:
25 minutes, plus marinating
Power setting:
HIGH
Cooking time:
15 minutes

DESSERTS & BAKING

MOROCCAN FRUIT COMPOTE

$2^{1}/_{2}$ *cups dried mixed fruits,*   *2 tablespoons honey*
  e.g. apricots, apples,   *1 cinnamon stick*
  pears, prunes or figs   *pinch of ground allspice*
$^{2}/_{3}$ *cup orange juice* $^{1}/_{4}$ *cup blanched almonds*
2 cups water

Serves 6
Preparation time:
5 minutes
Power setting:
HIGH
Cooking time:
15 minutes
Standing time:
Until cool

1. Place the fruits in a large bowl, pour in the orange juice and water, cover and cook on HIGH for 5 minutes.
2. Add the honey, cinnamon stick and allspice, cover and cook on HIGH for 10 minutes.
3. Leave to stand until cool, during which time the fruit will become plumper and more tender. Remove the cinnamon stick, stir in the almonds and chill until required. Serve with crisp biscuits.

CREME CARAMELS

$^{1}/_{2}$ *cup water* $^{1}/_{4}$ *cup superfine sugar*
$^{1}/_{2}$ *cup sugar*   *2 cups milk*
3 eggs   *1 teaspoon vanilla*
1 egg yolk

Serves 6
Preparation time:
10 minutes
Power setting:
HIGH and LOW
Cooking time:
27 minutes

1. Place the water and sugar in a heatproof glass jug and stir well. Cook on HIGH for 11 minutes, until golden; do not allow the syrup to become too brown, as it continues to cook after removal from the oven. Pour quickly into 6 ramekin dishes, then leave to cool and harden.
2. Meanwhile, beat the eggs, egg yolk and superfine sugar together.
3. Pour the milk into a jug and cook on HIGH for 4 minutes. Whisk into the egg mixture with the vanilla, then strain the mixture back into the jug. Divide between the dishes.
4. Stand the dishes in one container and pour in enough water to come halfway up the sides of the dishes. Cook on LOW for 12 minutes, until set.
5. Remove from the water, leave to cool, then chill.
6. To serve, invert each caramel onto a serving dish.

ORANGE SAVARIN

√

This impressive-looking cake, soaked in rum-flavored syrup, is a wonderful dessert for large gatherings.

FOR THE SAVARIN
  DOUGH:
½ cup butter
2 cups strong white flour
1 envelope active dry yeast
2 tablespoons superfine
  sugar
½ teaspoon salt
⅓ cup milk, warmed
3 eggs

FOR THE SYRUP:
¾ cup sugar
1¼ cups water
1 teaspoon lemon juice
⅓ cup orange juice
⅓ cup dark rum
TO FINISH:
¼ cup marmalade
⅔ cup whipping cream,
  whipped
3 large oranges, peeled and
  segmented

Serves 12–16
Preparation time:
42 minutes
Power setting:
HIGH
Cooking time:
18 minutes
Standing time:
10 minutes

1. Place the butter in a bowl and microwave on HIGH for 2 minutes.
2. Sift the flour, yeast, 1 tablespoon of the sugar and the salt into a large bowl. Make a well in the center and pour in the milk.
3. Beat the eggs and remaining sugar until frothy, then add to the flour with the melted butter and beat until smooth. Cover and leave for 10 minutes, then beat the dough with your hand for at least 2 minutes.
4. Spoon the dough into a greased 7½ cup ring mold and leave to rise in a warm place for about 30–40 minutes, until the mixture reaches the top of the mold.
5. Cook on HIGH for 7 minutes. Leave to stand for 10 minutes, then turn out onto a rack. Wash and dry the ring mold, then return the savarin to it.
6. To make the syrup, place the sugar and water in a bowl and microwave on HIGH for 8 minutes, until the sugar has dissolved. Cool until lukewarm, then stir in the fruit juices and rum.
7. Prick the savarin with a skewer and pour over the syrup. Leave to cool, then turn out onto a serving plate.
8. Place the marmalade in a bowl and microwave on HIGH for 1 minute, then brush over the outside of the savarin.
9. Pipe cream around the edge of the savarin and decorate with the orange segments.

TIPSY BREAD PUDDING ✓

*¹/₂ lb whole wheat bread,
    broken into pieces*
1 cup raisins
*¹/₃ cup light brown
    granulated sugar,
    packed*

pinch of mixed spice
¹/₄ cup dark rum
2 cups milk
¹/₄ cup butter
3 eggs beaten

1. Place the bread, raisins, half of the sugar and the mixed spice in a bowl.
2. Mix the rum and milk together, pour over the bread and leave to soak for 30 minutes.
3. Place the butter in a bowl and microwave on HIGH for 2 minutes.
4. Stir the beaten eggs and melted butter into the bread mixture, then pour into 4 or 6 greased ovenproof dishes. Cook on HIGH for 10 minutes.
5. Remove from the oven and sprinkle with the remaining sugar. Leave to stand for 2 minutes. Serve hot or cold with yogurt or whipped cream.

Serves 4–6
Preparation time:
10 minutes, plus
soaking time
Power setting:
HIGH
Cooking time:
12 minutes
Standing time:
2 minutes

CHRISTMAS PUDDING

All the family will love this traditional Christmas pudding, which is not too rich or heavy. Even though it cooks so quickly it can be made in advance and reheated when required.

³/4 cup all-purpose flour
pinch each of salt, nutmeg and cinnamon
1 teaspoon mixed spice
²/3 cup shredded suet
¹/2 cup fresh breadcrumbs
¹/3 cup dark brown sugar, packed
¹/3 cup mixed peel
¹/4 cup glace chopped cherries
¹/3 cup currants
1 cup golden raisins

1 cup raisins
1 cooking apple, peeled and chopped
¹/2 cup blanched, chopped almonds
grated rind and juice of ¹/2 lemon
grated rind and juice of 1 small orange
2 tablespoons brandy
2 eggs beaten
2 tablespoons molasses
2 tablespoons milk

Serves 6–8
Preparation time:
25 minutes, plus chilling time
Power setting:
HIGH
Cooking time:
10 minutes
Standing time:
10 minutes

1. Sift the flour, salt and spices together into a large bowl. Add the suet, breadcrumbs, sugar, peel, fruit and almonds, then beat in the remaining ingredients to form a soft dropping consistency. Cover and chill overnight.
2. Stir the mixture well, then place in a greased 5 cup pudding basin. Cover with greased waxed paper and secure with string or elastic band.
3. Cook on HIGH for 10 minutes. Leave to stand for 10 minutes before turning out.
4. To reheat, return pudding to the basin and cover with waxed paper. Cook on HIGH, allowing 1 minute per lb. Leave to stand for 1 minute before turning out.
5. Serve hot, decorated with holly leaves if wished, with whipped cream or brandy butter.

STRAWBERRY GALETTE

²/3 cup sweet butter
¹/2 cup powdered sugar, sifted
¹/4 teaspoon almond extract
1¹/2 cups all-purpose flour, sifted

¹/2 cup finely chopped blanched almonds
1 lb strawberries, halved
1¹/4 cups heavy cream, whipped
powdered sugar to dust

1. Cream the butter, powdered sugar and almond extract together in a bowl, then gradually work in the flour and almonds. Work the mixture until it binds together.
2. Divide the dough in half and press out to an 8 inch round on a piece of non-stick paper placed on the turntable. Prick all over and cook on LOW for 6 minutes. Leave to stand for 2 minutes.
3. Gently place an 8 inch round cake pan on top of the biscuit and, while it is still warm, neaten the edge with a sharp knife.
4. Repeat the cooking procedure with the second half of the dough. After neatening, cut this biscuit into 8 wedges. Leave both biscuits to cool.
5. Place the biscuit round on a flat serving plate and cover with half of the strawberries. Spread with the cream, then top with the remaining strawberries. Arrange the biscuit wedges on top and sprinkle with a little powdered sugar.

Serves 6
Preparation time:
25 minutes
Power setting:
LOW
Cooking time:
12 minutes
Standing time:
4 minutes

CONTINENTAL CHEESECAKE

This cake can be decorated with fruit of your choice. Serve thin slices as it is very rich.

1/4 cup butter
1/4 cup superfine sugar
3 tablespoons honey
2 eggs, beaten
2 cups curd cheese or
farmer's cheese
grated rind and juice of 1/2
lemon
2/3 cup sour cream
2 teaspoons cornstarch
1 teaspoon vanilla

1/3 cup golden raisins
FOR THE BASE:
1/4 cup butter
1 tablespoon golden syrup
or 1/2 tablespoon each
light corn syrup and
molasses
1/4 lb ginger snaps, crushed
TO DECORATE:
2/3 cup heavy cream,
whipped
slices of fruit, e.g. kiwi

Serves 10–12
Preparation time:
25 minutes
Power setting:
HIGH and
DEFROST
Cooking time:
21 minutes

1. Line the base and sides of a 6 cup microwave loaf dish with oiled waxed paper.
2. Beat together the butter, sugar and honey, then gradually add the eggs. Beat in the cheese, lemon rind and juice, sour cream, cornstarch and vanilla and mix until smooth. Fold in the golden raisins.
3. Spoon into prepared dish, cover with waxed paper and cook on DEFROST for 20 minutes. Remove cover.
4. Place the butter and syrup in a bowl and microwave on HIGH for 1 minute. Stir in the cookie crumbs, then spoon on top of the cheesecake, pressing down gently. Leave to cool then chill until required.
5. Invert the cake onto a serving plate and remove the waxed paper. Decorate with the cream and fruit.

BLUEBERRY TART

Blackberries, raspberries, strawberries and gooseberries go well with the creamy filling, too.

FOR THE PASTRY:
1 1/2 cups all-purpose flour
1/2 cup butter, cut into
small pieces
1/4 cup superfine sugar
grated rind and juice of 1
lemon

FOR THE FILLING:
1 cup low-fat Ricotta cheese
1 egg yolk
2/3 cup sour cream
4 cups blueberries
1/4 cup blackcurrant jelly
or conserve

1. Sift the flour into a bowl, then rub in the butter until the mixture resembles fine breadcrumbs. Stir in the sugar, add the lemon rind and enough juice to make a firm dough; knead well.

2. Roll out the pastry on a floured board and use to line a greased 9 inch fluted pie dish. Trim the edges and chill for 30 minutes.

3. Prick the base with a fork, then line the base with a double thickness of paper towels. Cook on HIGH for 3 minutes. Remove the paper towels and cook for 1½ minutes.

4. Beat the cheese, egg yolk and sour cream together, then pour into the flan case. Cook on LOW for 6 minutes or until set. Leave to cool.

5. Meanwhile, place the blueberries and jelly or conserve in a bowl and cook on HIGH for 3 minutes. Leave to cool, then spoon on top of the tart. Chill until set.

Serves 6–8
Preparation time:
30 minutes, plus chilling time
Power setting:
HIGH and LOW
Cooking time:
13½ minutes

CHOCOLATE FONDUE

√

Popular with adults and children, this is a scrumptious way to end a meal. Serve any selection of fruit in season to dip into the fondue.

¹/₂ lb Toblerone chocolate
²/₃ cup heavy cream

TO SERVE:
selection of fruit, sliced

Serves 6–8
Preparation time:
15 minutes
Power setting:
MEDIUM
Cooking time:
3 minutes

1. Break the chocolate into pieces and place in a bowl. Add the cream and microwave on MEDIUM for 3 minutes, stirring during cooking, until melted.
2. Pour the fondue into a bowl. Place the bowl on a large plate and arrange the slices of fruit attractively on the plate.

BLACKBERRY SYLLABUB   ✓

This delicious syllabub can be made using any soft fruit.

4 cups blackberries
½ cup sugar
2 tablespoons Crème de
  Cassis liqueur

1¼ cups heavy cream,
  whipped
1 egg white

1. Place the blackberries and sugar in a bowl, cover and cook on HIGH for 5 minutes.
2. Press the fruit through a sieve, discarding the seeds. Stir in the liqueur and leave to cool.
3. Fold in the cream.
4. Whisk the egg white until stiff, then fold into the syllabub. Pour into 6 glasses and chill until required.
5. Serve with dessert biscuits or ladies' fingers.

Serves 6
Preparation time:
15 minutes
Power setting:
HIGH
Cooking time:
5 minutes

√
BOOZY COFFEE RING

A favorite dessert for parties—it's easy to make and is always enjoyed by family and friends.

4 eggs
1/2 cup superfine sugar
1/4 cup butter
1 cup all-purpose flour
1 1/4 cups warm strong
  black coffee
2 tablespoons light brown
  granulated sugar,
  packed

1/4 cup brandy or Tia Maria
TO DECORATE:
1 1/4 cups whipping cream,
  whipped
1/4 cup slivered almonds,
  toasted (see page 7)

Serves 10–12
Preparation time:
25 minutes
Power setting:
HIGH
Cooking time:
6 minutes
Standing time:
10 minutes

1. Whisk the eggs and superfine sugar together until very light and fluffy and about trebled in volume.
2. Place the butter in a bowl and microwave on HIGH for 1 minute.
3. Sift the flour over the egg mixture, then pour in the butter in a slow stream. Fold in carefully with a metal spoon, then pour into a greased 7 1/2 cup ring mold.
4. Cook on HIGH for 5 minutes. Leave to stand for 10 minutes, then turn out onto a rack to cool.
5. Return the cake to the cleaned ring mold and prick with a skewer.
6. Mix the coffee and light brown sugar together, stirring to dissolve the sugar. Stir in the brandy or Tia Maria, pour over the cake and leave to soak.
7. Turn out the cake onto a serving plate and cover with the cream. Sprinkle with the almonds.

√
APPLE AND RASPBERRY CHARLOTTE

A family favorite, this dessert could be made with black-berries or boysenberries instead of raspberries.

1 1/2 lb cooking apples,
  peeled and chopped
1/4 cup sugar, or to taste
3/4 lb raspberries, thawed if
  frozen
1/4 cup butter

4 cups whole wheat
  breadcrumbs
1/3 cup light brown sugar,
  packed
2/3 cup heavy cream,
  whipped
1/4 cup chopped walnuts

1. Place the apples in a bowl with 3 tablespoons water, cover and cook on HIGH for 5 minutes, stirring halfway through cooking.

2. Add the sugar and mash with a fork. Leave to cool, then stir in the raspberries.

3. Place the butter in a large heatproof glass dish and microwave on HIGH for 1 minute. Stir in the breadcrumbs and brown sugar, spreading out evenly. Cook on HIGH for 10 to 12 minutes, stirring every minute during cooking. Leave to cool, allowing the crumbs to become crisp.

4. Spread one third of the crumbs onto the base of a glass bowl. Cover with half of the fruit. Sprinkle with half of the remaining crumbs, then the remaining fruit. Finish with a layer of crumbs.

5. Pipe the cream around the edge of the charlotte and sprinkle with the nuts. Serve as soon as possible.

Serves 6–8
Preparation time:
15 minutes
Power setting:
HIGH
Cooking time:
18 minutes

DATE FLAPJACKS

*1¹/₃ cups dates, pitted and
    chopped*
¹/₄ cup water
¹/₃ cup margarine
*1 tablespoon golden syrup
    or ¹/₂ tablespoon each
    light corn syrup and
    molasses*

*¹/₄ cup light brown
    granulated sugar,
    packed*
1 cup porridge oats
1 cup whole wheat flour

Makes 8
Preparation time:
15 minutes
Power setting:
HIGH
Cooking time:
10 minutes

1. Place the dates and water in a bowl, cover and cook on HIGH for 3 minutes. Mash the soft dates with a fork, adding a little more water if they are too dry to make a spreading consistency.
2. Place the margarine, syrup and sugar in a bowl and microwave on HIGH for 2 minutes, until the margarine has melted. Mix in the oats and flour.
3. Spread one half of the oat mixture over the base of a 7 inch pie plate, then cover with the dates, spreading evenly. Spoon the remaining oat mixture on top and press down well.
4. Cook on HIGH for 5 minutes. Cut into wedges, while still slightly warm. Leave until cold, then remove the flapjacks from the dish.

BANANA AND CHOCOLATE CHIP CAKE

¹/₂ cup margarine
*¹/₂ cup light brown sugar,
    packed*
2 eggs, beaten

2 large bananas
2 cups self-rising flour
1 teaspoon baking powder
¹/₃ cup chocolate chips

Serves 8–10
Preparation time:
15 minutes
Power setting:
HIGH
Cooking time:
7 minutes
Standing time:
3 minutes

1. Place the margarine and sugar in a bowl and beat together until light and creamy. Beat in the eggs one at a time.
2. Mash the bananas and beat into the cake mixture.
3. Sift the flour and baking powder together. Fold into the cake mixture with the chocolate chips.
4. Spoon the mixture into a greased 7¹/₂ cup microwave ring mold and cook on HIGH for 7 minutes.
5. Leave to stand for 3 minutes, then turn out and cool on a rack.

MINCEMEAT CAKE

Mincemeat gives this cake a delicious, moist flavor. Split and fill with buttercream if you prefer a richer cake.

2 cups all-purpose flour
2 teaspoons baking
   powder
1/2 teaspoon baking soda
3/4 cup light brown sugar,
   packed
1/2 cup butter
2/3 cup plain yogurt
2 eggs, beaten

grated rind of 1 lemon
1/2 cup mincemeat
TO DECORATE:
1 cup powdered sugar,
   sifted
3 teaspoons lemon juice
angelica
crystallized lemon slices

Makes one 8 inch cake
Preparation time:
20 minutes
Power setting:
HIGH
Cooking time:
10 minutes
Standing time:
5 minutes

1. Sift the flour, baking powder and baking soda into a bowl, then stir in the sugar.
2. Place the butter in a bowl and microwave on HIGH for 1 minute. Beat into the flour with the yogurt to make a smooth batter. Gradually beat in the eggs and lemon rind, then add the mincemeat.
3. Turn the mixture into a greased deep 8 inch cake dish and cook on HIGH for 8–9 minutes. Leave to stand for 5 minutes, then turn out onto a rack to cool.
4. Beat the powdered sugar and lemon juice together to make a thick glace icing. Spread over the top of the cake and decorate with angelica and lemon slices.

ICED GINGERBREAD

Whole wheat flour gives this cake a nuttier texture. Try adding some raisins or chopped preserved ginger to the mixture.

3/4 cup margarine
1/4 cup golden syrup or 2
   tablespoons each light
   corn syrup and molasses
1/4 cup molasses
1/3 cup dark brown sugar,
   packed
3 cups whole wheat flour
1 tablespoon each ground
   ginger and baking
   powder

1 teaspoon baking soda
1 teaspoon salt
1 egg, beaten
1 1/4 cups milk
TO DECORATE:
2 cups powdered sugar,
   sifted
2 tablespoons water
2 oz crystallized ginger,
   chopped

1. Grease and line the base of an $8\frac{1}{2}$ inch square dish.
2. Place the margarine, syrup, molasses and sugar in a bowl and microwave on HIGH for 2 minutes, until the margarine has melted.
3. Place the flour in a large bowl, then sift in the ginger, baking powder, baking soda and salt. Beat in the egg, milk and melted mixture.
4. Pour into the prepared dish and cook on HIGH for 12 minutes. Leave to stand for 10 minutes, then turn out onto a rack to cool.
5. Beat the powdered sugar with the water to make a thick glace icing, then spread over the top of the cake. Sprinkle with the chopped ginger. Cool; then cut into fingers.

Makes one $8\frac{1}{2}$ inch cake
Preparation time: 15 minutes
Power setting: HIGH
Cooking time: 14 minutes
Standing time: 10 minutes

CHOCOLATE COCONUT BROWNIES

These are so quick you can make them within minutes of children arriving home with unexpected friends for an after-school snack.

1¹/₄ cups whole wheat flour
1¹/₂ teaspoons baking powder
¹/₂ teaspoon baking soda
³/₄ cup light brown sugar, packed

1¹/₃ cups desiccated coconut
¹/₄ cup cocoa powder
¹/₂ cup margarine, diced
2 eggs, beaten
²/₃ cup milk

Makes 16
Preparation time:
10 minutes
Power setting:
HIGH
Cooking time:
9 minutes
Standing time:
5 minutes

1. Grease and line an 8½ inch square dish.
2. Mix together the flour, baking powder, baking soda, sugar, coconut and cocoa in a large bowl.
3. Place the margarine in a bowl and microwave on HIGH for 1 minute. Beat into the dry ingredients, with the eggs and milk, until smooth. Pour into the prepared dish.
4. Cook on HIGH for 8 minutes. Leave to stand for 5 minutes, then turn out onto a rack to cool.
5. Cut into squares to serve.

APPLE AND WALNUT LOAF

1¹/₂ cups whole wheat flour
1 teaspoon baking powder
¹/₂ teaspoon mixed spice
¹/₃ cup margarine
¹/₂ cup light brown sugar, packed

1 egg, beaten
¹/₂ lb cooking apples, peeled and grated coarsely
¹/₂ cup chopped walnuts
3 tablespoons milk

Makes 10 slices
Preparation time:
15 minutes
Power setting:
HIGH
Cooking time:
5 minutes
Standing time:
10 minutes

1. Place the flour, baking powder and mixed spice in a bowl, mix together and set aside.
2. Beat the margarine and three-quarters of the light brown sugar together until creamy, then add the egg, beating well.
3. Fold in the flour mixture, then the apple and walnuts. Stir in the milk.
4. Turn the mixture into a greased 5 × 7 inch loaf dish, level the top, then sprinkle with the remaining brown sugar.
5. Cook on HIGH for 5 minutes. Leave to stand for 10 minutes, then turn out onto a rack to cool. Cut into slices to serve. Best eaten same day as making.

INDEX

Photography by: Martin Brigdale
Designed by: Sue Storey
Home economist: Lorna Rhodes
Stylist: Liz Hippisley
Jacket photograph by: Paul Williams
Illustration by: Linda Smith
U.S. Consultant Editor: Carla Capalbo